USING GPS

Conrad Dixon

**SHERIDAN
HOUSE**

This edition
first published 1994 by
Sheridan House Inc.
145 Palisade Street
Dobbs Ferry, NY 10522

Library of Congress Cataloging-in-Publication Data

Dixon, Conrad.
    Using GPS / Conrad Dixon.
       p.   cm.
    ISBN 0-924486-70-8: $14.95
    1. Global Positioning System. 2. Yachts and yachting. I. Title.
VK562. D59 1994   94-5802
623. 89'3- -dc20   CIP

Printed in the United Kingdom

ISBN 0-924486-70-8

Contents

Acknowledgements

I am most grateful to Michael J Mitchell of Raytheon in the United States for the loan of an Echostar 790 and also for providing a colour slide and photograph of the product. Also, my thanks go to Marianne Rasmussen of Raytheon's headquarters in England for supplying photographs.

Kristen Ehrlich of Micrologic in California was kind enough to clear the way for access to an Admiral set, and sent an illustration, while Patrick Cooney of A–1 Marine, Fort Lauderdale, was most helpful in supplying the Admiral unit.

Jim White of Magellan in California took a great deal of trouble to make a 5000D set available, and also sent photographs. Helen Knight and Ken Carter of Trimble at Hook in Hampshire provided information and illustrations, as did Richard Williams of Streamline in Surbiton and Kathe Wood of Garmin in Lenexa, Kansas.

My sincere thanks to all of you for your help.

CONRAD DIXON

1 How GPS works

The Global Positioning System is a satellite-based radio-navigation network that provides fixes in all parts of the world at all times of the day and night. Developed and operated by the US Department of Defense, it is based on a space segment of 24 satellites in circular orbits about 10 900 nautical miles above the earth's surface. These satellites are so spaced that usually about five of them are in theoretical view of any user at any one time. Each satellite goes round the world twice a day in one of six planes, and transmits two kinds of data in two different digital codes continuously. The control segment consists of a master station at Colorado Springs and a number of monitor stations that track those satellites in view and act as conduits for information passing between them and the master station. The purpose of this information exchange is to enable the satellite to transmit an accurately timed signal to a receiver. The time interval is turned into a distance, and thus becomes a position line. Satellites are fitted with atomic clocks to record the precise time a signal is sent, and the transmission times are computed by the receiver, employed to solve a fairly simple geometric equation leading to a fix, which is then displayed for navigation purposes.

The position line, or line of range on the surface of the earth, is crossed with others to give a fix. Three position lines give what is called a 2D fix: four will give a 3D fix that takes account of altitude. Normally, you will be operating a set whose antenna height is always the same, and that is allowed for when installation and initialization take place, but use at home or from high ground may

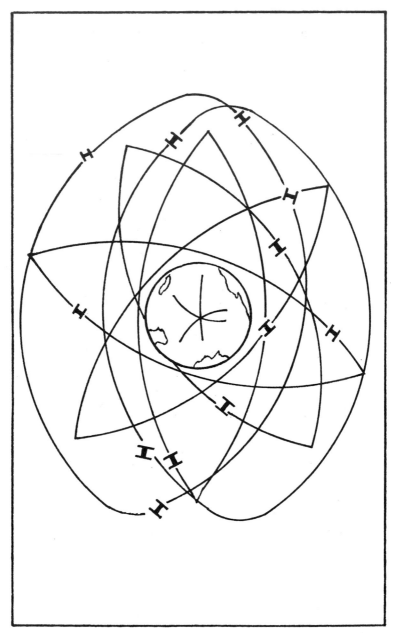

Fig 1. Satellites providing a fix.

entail telling the set how far it is above sea level to improve accuracy. The functioning of GPS is outlined in Fig 1, where a 'birdcage' of orbits and satellite vehicles encloses the earth and a fix from three ranges appears on it. Satellites look a little like cotton reels flanked by playing cards, and the latter element is the framework for solar panels that provide operating power. Technically minded readers may care to know that transmission times are recorded in nanoseconds (millionths of a second), and that atomic clocks in satellites have about one second of error in 70 000 years. Transmission takes place on 1575.42 MHz and 1227.6 MHz, with the former wavelength carrying what are called pseudo-random code messages for civilian use. The pseudo-random codes give the time difference between transmission and reception, and Fig 2 shows how the receiving set (marked with an R) compares the message from the satellite with an internally generated version to get the time difference – TD. This time is converted to a range, so that – as with radar – intersecting arcs of range provide a fix.

SOURCES OF ERROR

The speed of radio signals, which is the same as the speed of light, is only constant in a vacuum, and messages tend to slow down as they pass through the ionosphere about a hundred miles above the earth. A similar delay takes place as signals pass through the atmosphere, where water vapour has a braking effect. Fortunately, these factors only give a few metres of error, but the angles of intercept are more significant. Plotting conventional bearings on a chart gives best results when the lines of bearing are at right angles, and the same applies with satellite ranges. Wide angles give the best results and, although the computer part of a set is programmed to select angles to get the best fix, there are occasions when the operator will want to know for himself or herself if the geometry is such that good results can be obtained. Fig 3 depicts good geometry and bad, with what is called a low HDOP (Horizontal Dilution of Precision) to the left of the diagram. HDOP is simply a measure of expected fix accuracy from the satellites being tracked, and examples will be given in Chapter 4. For the moment, assimilate the idea that if the satellites are closely bunched the position fix will be a poor one, and the HDOP number will be higher. Typically, an HDOP number such as 02 is good news, while a number such as 07 is suspect. Sometimes, the expressions Geometric Quality (GQ) and Geometric Dilution of Precision (GDOP) are used to describe satellite status; these terms mean the same thing, although this time the low numbers are suspect, with 7–9 being good and 0–3 signalling unreliable fixes.

SIGNAL QUALITY

Whereas Dilution of Precision (DOP) is all about the placing of satellites, Signal Quality (SQ) relates to the strength of signals from an individual satellite. The SQ number is an indication of the carrier-to-noise or signal-to-noise ratio, with 7–9 meaning strong signals and 0–3 being so weak as to be liable to lose lock. A GPS satellite that has developed a technical fault is declared 'unhealthy', and its transmissions are coded as unusable so that receiving sets ignore them. Some sets have a graphical representation of SQ by bar chart or with numerical data given alongside each satellite identification number, and we'll look at the practical aspect of SQ information in Chapter 4.

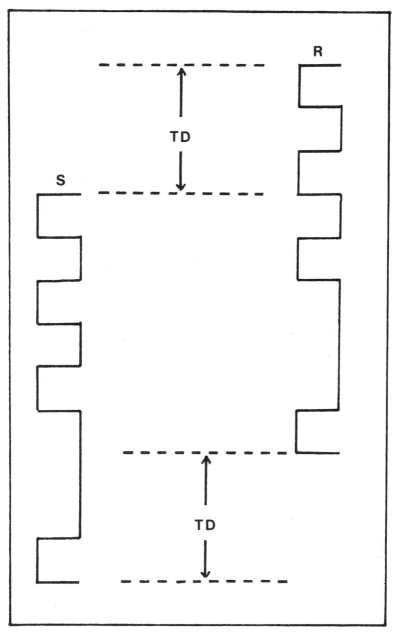

Fig 2. Pseudo-random codes compared.

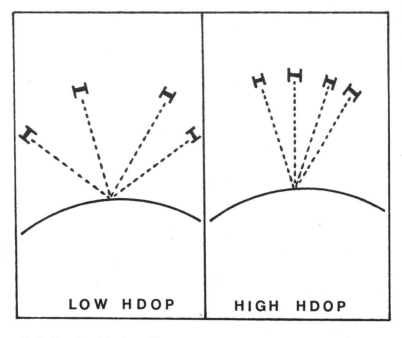

Fig 3. Good and bad satellite geometry.

THE TWO CODES AND SELECTIVE AVAILABILITY

It was stated earlier that satellites transmit two kinds of data in two different codes. One tranche of data is called the Almanac and relates to the health of the satellite, while the second is Ephemeris data about the precise orbital parameters of the satellite and hence the range to a terrestrial position. The information is put in one of two codes: the very accurate Protected (or Precision) Code (P-Code) is for military use, and the 'unprotected' Coarse (or Course) Acquisition code (C/A) is what *we* get on our sets. The master station can, and does, degrade the accuracy of the signals by means of variable adjustments, so that 95 per cent of the time the position given by your set is within a 100-metre radius of the true position, while the other 5 per cent of the time it will be outside that circle. The euphemism for this deliberate degradation of accuracy is Selective Availability, and we shall see later that both users of GPS and manufacturers of sets devote a great deal of time and ingenuity to circumventing the constraints of Selective Availability in order to get results similar to those provided by the P-Code. The modified civilian system that seeks to emulate military precision is called Differential Global Positioning System (DGPS), and some of the sets we will be looking at are constructed to take advantage of a development that is likely to give a fix with an average accuracy radius of between 5 and 10 metres.

At the time of writing, the US Department of Defense had the ability to switch off GPS altogether, and it has done so on two occasions during the short period that the system has been available for civilian use. It was 'out' for some hours during the Gulf War, and seven satellites were switched off for seven hours during a public holiday in the United States in 1992. It must always be borne in mind that war, civil unrest or terrorist threats may cause the suspension of transmissions without warning, and that undue reliance on a single source of navigational information is unwise. It should also be appreciated that grumbling about Selective Availability is a little churlish because, after all, we don't actually pay anything for using a system that was developed for Cold War purposes and has now been made freely available to a wide spectrum of users.

2 GPS sets and their installation

POWER AND COMPATIBILITY

There are two main types of sets, fixed and hand-held, and the principal difference between them is that the former run on the boat's batteries and the latter on torch or shaver batteries that require fairly frequent renewal. It follows that if a navigator wants to link his GPS set with a number of other electronic devices such as a plotter, digitized chart, radar or autopilot, he must either choose a fixed set powered from 12-volt batteries and replenished from the motor, or convert the hand-held to a fixed set by putting it on a bracket or mount and getting power from the same 12-volt source via an adaptor while bypassing the alkaline or NiCad torch batteries. Attempts to run a number of units from these small batteries will often result in the hand-held set refusing duty or giving a low power signal. There is, however, another lithium battery in most sets that may be soldered in position and difficult to replace. It powers the memory that stores data when the unit has been unplugged and taken home for winter storage, and this battery will last up to five years. Replacement should be carried out by the dealer who sold you the set, and it is a good idea to get this battery changed about every third year to ensure trouble-free operation.

An American organization called the National Maritime Electronics Association (NMEA) sets world standards for the compatibility of electronic equipment; this means, for example, that if your GPS set bears an NMEA 0183 label it will work with an autopilot bearing the same number. Some units will be compatible with more than one NMEA number, and in Chapter 8 we will look at the procedure to be followed when connecting the GPS set to another electronic device.

THE SETS

Five sets are studied in this book: the first two are hand-held and the remainder are fixed units. The words in brackets below are the abbreviated names of the sets; these are the names that will be used in the text here-after:

Maker or supplier	Set name	Abbreviated name
Garmin International Inc, 9875 Widmer Road, Lenexa, KS 66215, USA	GPS75	(Garmin)
Magellan Systems Corp, 960 Overland Court, San Dimas, CA 91773, USA	GPS NAV 5000D	(Magellan)
Apelco Marine Electronics Co, 46 River Road, Hudson, NH 03051, USA	GXL 1100 GPS	(Apelco)
Raytheon Marine Sales and Service, Elizabeth Way, The Pinnacles, Harlow, Essex, CM19 5AZ	Raytheon Echostar 790	(Echostar)
Micrologic, 9610 DeSoto Avenue, Chatsworth, CA 91311, USA	Admiral GPS	(Admiral)

There is a further subdivision of function and operation within these five sets. The Echostar is a combined GPS set, fish finder and plotter, while the Admiral has many thousands of lights and buoys in its memory in waypoint form. The Garmin and Echostar have simulators for 'dummy runs' at home, the Magellan and Garmin have

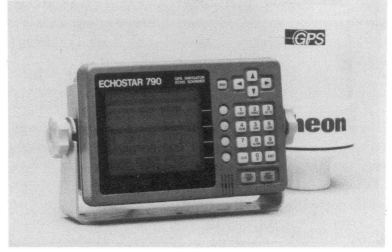

Raytheon's Echostar 790 GPS fish finder/plotter.

built-in antennae, and the Apelco and Echostar have a separate sensor with the receiver and antenna combined. Installation of the antenna should precede anything else, because so many faults may be attributed to incorrect positioning.

ANTENNA INSTALLATION

The first principle is that a GPS set likes a clear horizon, but does *not* need to have the antenna as high as possible. The signals may become unreliable close to tall structures, under trees, masts, sails, rigging, deckhouses or inside buildings, and if you want to test on land it is best to go to a bare hill and either take an extra cable and plug to power the set from the cigarette lighter socket in your car, or carry a 12-volt lantern battery with you. At sea, the antenna for a set fitted in a sailing boat will work best on the pushpit in a position at least a metre clear of other aerials, and *not* in the path of the radar beam. Mast-top mounting should be avoided, for pitch and roll will cause

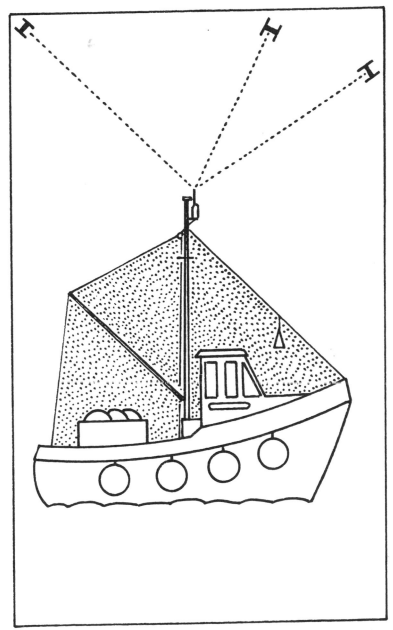

Fig 4. Poor reception in shaded area.

constant small corrections to position figures and, in most cases, the VHF aerial has got there first.

In motor craft the antenna needs to be above structures that might interfere with line-of-sight reception, and in Figure 4 it can be seen mounted clear of all the shaded area where interference is likely. Similar considerations apply when using a hand-held set, for although it does not require a separate antenna the set will work best when the signal is unimpeded. If you can envisage two crewmen holding sets on an upper and a lower deck simultaneously, it is obvious that the 'upstairs' hand-held set has a better chance of receiving quality signals. Hand-held sets may, paradoxically, work best when not held in the hand, for if they are wedged into a holder with the built-in aerial high enough for good reception, the operator can key with one hand and write with the other. Some owners clove hitch a piece of cord around the waist of their hand-helds so that they can be lashed to something solid in rough weather, and it does not matter if the set is laid flat so long as the antenna is raised in the upright position. The Magellan is the best one for rough weather because it is waterproof and has a rubbery skin that clings to a sloping surface despite the plunging and rolling of the boat.

FITTING THE SET

Fixed sets need to be accessible and protected from the weather, and in motor craft they are commonly fitted to the console. Make sure that there are no hidden wires or current-carrying instruments behind the selected site and try to leave seven inches of free space all around it. This is hard to achieve in many small yachts, but you should at least position the GPS set a minimum of twenty inches away from a magnetic compass. Before screwing every-thing down, experiment by trying all the potential positions within reach of the power and antenna cables, and check that it's going to work. With the Admiral, the procedure goes something like this. Connect the antenna cable to the fitting at the back of the set marked ANTENNA INPUT. Turn all other electrical or electronic units off before connecting the power plug to J2 – a port at the back of the set. Press the ON/OFF switch at the front of the set. The screen should illuminate and shift to a message saying ACQUIRING SATELLITES/DATA. Then switch off – you've proved it's going to work in the chosen position.

In sailing craft the set is often mounted at the navigator's work station on a bulkhead above the chart table, and a short-handed or racing crew may need to have an on-deck repeater to save constant trips up and down the companion to see what's going on. All fixed sets will need grounding to receive interference-free signals, and this is normally done in steel craft by running a wire strop from the butterfly nut at the back of the set to the hull. With a glassfibre yacht the wire strop goes to the engine block or to a ground plate below the waterline. This ground wire 'draws' unwanted noise interference away from the receiver and also provides some protection during electrical storms or lightning strikes. Finally, there is the antenna to consider. In a sailing boat this is often left out in the wind and rain for years on end, and such benign neglect is exactly the right policy. Whatever you do, *don't* paint it – if you do, it will never work properly again. If you feel the antenna should be taken home in winter with the set, then remember that a dry wipe is the only attention it needs.

ESSENTIAL PRELIMINARIES

People who are unfamiliar with machines worry about two aspects of their use – keying, and making mistakes. The first thing to grasp is that GPS sets have two types of keys. 'Hard' keys generally have a single function, and the convention is that when they are described in an instruction manual, or in this book, they are shown boxed, as with ENT and CLR. 'Soft' keys are adjacent to a page or display and are often blank because they have numerous functions. What they do is shown in unboxed capitals, and when an invitation such as NAVIGATE or STEER appears on the screen, then the softkey nearest the item, and often pointed to with an arrow, is the one to be touched.

The Garmin GPS 75.

Mis-keying is a common error when a set is in use, and the Garmin will let you CLR a single wrong entry while other sets use a CLR to wipe out the whole thing. A sophisticated set like the Echostar provides you with more options. A single digit error is corrected by using REV to go back one space, and a CLR will blot it out. If you go hopelessly wrong, the Echostar is programmed so that a touch of $\boxed{\text{MODE}}$ allows you to go back to the beginning, while the Apelco has $\boxed{\text{EXIT}}$ for the same purpose. The up-and-down and right-and-left arrows serve to divide functions into groups and specifics, and as a general rule $\boxed{\triangle}$ and $\boxed{\triangledown}$ make a shift between groups while $\boxed{\triangleright}$ and $\boxed{\triangleleft}$ enable the user to scroll between specific items. For example, with the Magellan, a search for a particular waypoint on the list starts at $\boxed{\text{WPT}}$, with repeated touches on $\boxed{\triangleright}$ giving them in ascending numerical order. Turning off a set may require two key presses simultaneously, and the Apelco needs $\boxed{\text{ENTER/POWER}}$ and $\boxed{\text{CLEAR/OFF}}$ together in order to stop work: the reason being that two key touches are deliberate, but one could be accidental. Finally, let us not forget the most-used key of them all: $\boxed{\text{ENT}}$ or $\boxed{\text{ENTER}}$ is the confirmation key for instructions and cancellations, and almost every input finishes with this key.

3 Start-up and early problems

The first television sets required a period of time to warm up after being switched on, and unprepared GPS sets may take from three to twenty minutes to provide a position fix from a cold start. However, if the GPS set is told roughly where it is on the surface of the earth, it should supply the first position fix in one or two minutes. This first start, or initialization process, entails entering the approximate latitude and longitude of present position, plus altitude, date and time where appropriate; this has to be done when the set is new or at the beginning of the season where present location is more than a hundred miles from where the set was last used. When a set is going to be used at the same place as where it was turned off in the autumn, it should readily reacquire signals without intialization, but if a flashing display persists for some minutes this is a sure sign that the start-up routine must be followed. This important first step will be illustrated by three examples.

FIRST START – ADMIRAL

Press $\boxed{\text{ON/OFF}}$ for one second, and then go to:

$\boxed{\text{MENU}}$ $\boxed{\text{MENU}}$ and repeated $\boxed{+}$ or $\boxed{-}$ scrolling

until FIRST START PROCEDURE appears on the screen. An $\boxed{\text{ENT}}$ will produce detailed instructions.

The display tells you to HOLD CLR DOWN 10 SEC, and after that time a PROCEDURE block appears telling you to enter various pieces of data, starting with time

Micrologic Admiral GPS set

zone. Imagine you are in Florida where the time zone is +5 hours on Greenwich; you need to touch:

$\boxed{+}$ $\boxed{5}$

followed by local time, date and approximate latitude and longitude as the flashing cursor moves on. (Here I must digress to explain about the latitude and longitude entry. Leading zeroes are necessary where the whole latitude and longitude figures are small ones, while minutes are entered as whole numbers followed by an imaginary decimal point and thousandths of a minute from 001 to 999 with this particular set.) As we are dealing with an approximate latitude and longitude in this instance, the keying continues:

$\boxed{2}\boxed{4}$ $\boxed{0}\boxed{0}$ $\boxed{0}\boxed{0}\boxed{0}$ $\boxed{ENT}$

$\boxed{0}\boxed{8}\boxed{0}$ $\boxed{0}\boxed{0}$ $\boxed{0}\boxed{0}\boxed{0}$ $\boxed{ENT}$

Altitude is the next item. The antenna on the pushpit is approximately 6 feet above sea level, so that:

$$\boxed{6} \quad \boxed{\text{ENT}}$$

is needed. The start-up procedure is completed with a READY on a softkey, and the next press of $\boxed{\text{POS}}$ should give latitude and longitude of present position after a brief acquisition interval.

Navigators are renowned as doubting Thomases, so if you want to check that this start-up has 'taken', just touch the right-hand softkey under the screen that gives TIME. The page should then look something like this:

Time Zone / Day Light	
EASTERN STANDARD	+ 5 hrs
LOCAL TIME	Thursday
16:52:53	10
	March 1994
UTC / GMT	
21:52:53	

– with a number of blanks and the ETA slot showing local time.

INITIALIZATION – MAGELLAN

If you buy a new Magellan, it arrives with batteries fitted and the Battery Saver ON so that you can go straight into action. In this example, the set is being operated from a hill in central southern England where the approximate latitude is 51°N and the longitude 1° 30'W. The altitude is 160 feet. Note that while latitude and longitude need to be within a hundred miles or so, the height should be as exact as you can get it using an Ordnance Survey map. If you forget to put in the altitude, the set will assume a zero elevation, and this is hardly ever the case on land or at sea. The work begins:

| ON/OFF | | SET UP | | ▽ | | ▽ | | ▽ | | ▽ | | ▽ | | ▽ | | ▽ |

to get an INIT display on which you put the latitude and longitude as:

| 5 | | 1 | | 0 | | 0 | | 0 | | 0 | | ENTER |

| 0 | | 0 | | 1 | | 3 | | 0 | | 0 | | 0 | | ENTER | | ▽ |

and the invitation to ENTER ELEVATION appears. Touch in:

| 1 | | 6 | | 0 | | ENTER | | ▽ | and INIT TIME comes up.

If you want to operate in UTC/GMT (and that is best with this set), do absolutely nothing because the unit will either be showing it already or it will come up with the first POS when satellite signals are being acquired. Naturally, if the machine suffers a memory loss or is used more than a hundred miles from the last fix, you should go through initialization again. If orthodox initialization fails (usually through mis-keying and putting in a grossly incorrect latitude and longitude), you can always touch AUX 5 ENTER to start Sky Search – a random hunt for satellites. Sky Search will give a fix in about 15 minutes, but this procedure is heavy on the batteries. When the Battery Saver is ON, the set turns itself off every two minutes when nothing much is happening, and to go to continuous operation key:

$\boxed{\text{AUX}}$ $\boxed{\triangleright}$ × 10 and then another $\boxed{\triangleright}$

to change BATTERY SAVER to BATTERY SAVER
ON   OFF

The battery warning to signal that six new AA alkaline batteries are needed takes two forms. The first is a battery symbol on the page; the second is the blunt admonition REPLACE BATTS OR LOSE DATA. With luck, the batteries should last about ten hours.

ECHOSTAR START-UP

The same principles apply to the Echostar, which needs to be told the approximate latitude and longitude, the antenna height, and date and time. Start with $\boxed{\text{MODE}}$ and the GPS softkey. Select SATELLITE STATUS and EST (for estimated position) on the softkey. (As it happens, all these items are on the same softkey, which makes life easy.) The instruction on the page now reads ENTER YOUR LATITUDE. In this example, the yacht is at sea off Fort Everglades where the approximate figures are 25°N and 80° 2'W, so that the keying is:

$\boxed{2}$ $\boxed{5}$ $\boxed{0}$ $\boxed{0}$ $\boxed{0}$ $\boxed{0}$ $\boxed{\text{ENT}}$ and

$\boxed{0}$ $\boxed{8}$ $\boxed{0}$ $\boxed{0}$ $\boxed{2}$ $\boxed{0}$ $\boxed{0}$ $\boxed{\text{ENT}}$

The instruction follows to put in antenna height, which is calculated with this set in metres, so that the next item is:

$\boxed{0}$ $\boxed{2}$ $\boxed{\text{ENT}}$

Now for date and time; these go in *backwards* with the year first:

9   4   0   3   2   7   ENT

The above example stands for 27 March 1994. You may be wondering why the information is in this order? The reason is that GPS development is, in racing terms, by American know-how out of Japanese chips, and the American way of citing dates is by month followed by day: giving them as March 27 rather than the usual British format of 27 March. Time goes in by standard 24-hour notation as:

0   4   3   8   ENT

standing for the UTC/GMT equivalent of a local time of 9.38 am.

Next, touch the NAV softkey and check that the data entered is correct. The Echostar will memorize this information and, provided that you use the set every hundred miles or so, will acquire and process fresh satellite data in a couple of minutes. It therefore pays to use your GPS set every now and again even though you know exactly where you are, in order to compel an update at intervals.

EAST OF GREENWICH, SOUTH OF THE EQUATOR

Sets reach their users with north latitude and west longitude appearing on the display at first operation, and if you start off east of the Greenwich meridian or south of the Equator a manual correction is necessary. The Apelco has a key with two semi-circular arrows on it for changing hemisphere designation, while the Garmin goes from N to S and W to E with pressings of $\boxed{\text{CLR}}$ confirmed with $\boxed{\text{ENT}}$. The Admiral has a $\boxed{\text{S } \nabla \text{ E}}$ key for the change, while the Magellan is typical of many sets in allowing the change to be made as the latitude and longitude go in during initialization. You key in the latitude numbers and press $\boxed{\triangleright}$ and $\boxed{\text{ENTER}}$ to change N to S. Similarly, after keying the longitude figures, touch $\boxed{\triangleright}$ and $\boxed{\text{ENTER}}$ to change W to E.

EAST/WEST ERROR

When cruising in the English Channel and close to the Greenwich meridian, it will be necessary to change back from E to W when passing between Newhaven and Brighton on the English side and Le Havre and Ouistreham on the French coast. Failure to make the change leads to east/west error – the cause of much discomfort among navigators. Mediterranean sailors must be prepared to change the hemisphere sign quite often when voyaging up and down Spain's east coast, and north/south error is a common operating mistake when sailing from the South China to the Java Sea or heading for Tahiti from the west coast of the United States. Fortunately, the very magnitude of the error soon tells the navigator how he has gone wrong.

NO USEFUL SIGNAL

The most disconcerting thing that can happen after initialization is to get a meaningless response, and an example of this follows. The $\boxed{\text{POS}}$ key is pressed on an Admiral and, after the usual short delay, the set comes up with SATS REC'D 0/5 and ACC 9999 ft. This tells you that although five satellites are theoretically on call, not one of them is being received, while the 9999 figure suggests that a fix cannot be computed. The Sky Plot that comes up with POS can confirm the azimuth (direction) and elevation of each satellite, so what has gone wrong? There are two possibilities. If you have mis-keyed the latitude and longitude figures, the initialization process has not 'taken' and will have to be done again. Second, the position of the antenna may not be correct. Perhaps it is not vertical, or it may be in the 'shadow' of something substantial so that signals are blocked, or it could be that it is not properly connected. If the set is working but not giving useful information, the two things to do are to go through initialization again and juggle with the antenna. With a hand-held set it is often just a question of moving a few feet one way or the other to get a clearer 'view' of the satellites.

TRUE OR MAGNETIC?

Most GPS sets leave the factory programmed to give courses and bearing in relation to magnetic north and taking account of changes in variation automatically. The mode is termed Auto Mag, and if a navigator wants to be in a position to use true courses and bearings to match figures given by a fluxgate compass he must make a manual correction. With the Apelco, the task is relatively simple. Touch SET UP and ENTER ENTER ENTER until the MAG page appears. It will look something like this:

```
                    MAG

        Ent                    VAR

        W 08°
```

The ⟳ key will prepare the set for manual entry, and by putting in zeroes and another ENTER, the future bearings and courses displayed will be true. Operators *can* put variation in manually, but Auto Mag is generally more reliable and less prone to interpretation errors than the human being. GPS sets have built-in klutz resistance, and it is wiser to believe that the machine knows best.

4 Position and status

The principal function of a GPS set is to give position, and while many sets require a press of POS there are some that give it automatically after switch-on. The Garmin starts work with a touch of PWR/STAT , and after conducting a series of self-tests it displays an advertising message followed by a graphical display of Signal Quality (SQ) for each visible satellite looking like this:

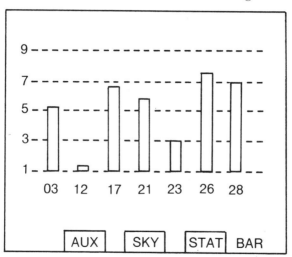

The numbers on the left-hand side of the page give SQ on a scale of 1 to 9, with the low numbers indicating weak signals. The row of numbers near the bottom are Satellite Information Numbers (SINs) that identify each one, while the bars on the chart show which ones are going to prove useful and those that are too feeble for use. As you can see, satellite 12 is not much use but the rest are giving a good signal for a fix. The boxed items at the foot of the display relate to softkey options on keys immediately

beneath them, and we will return to their function after
we have finished plotting the position. At this stage, all
we need to do with the Garmin is precisely nothing, for
when acquisition is complete the position page appears
in the following form:

```
TRK      218°     6kt

N        50°      22.328'

W        002°     31.245'

Altitude          11ft


        PLOT    CDI    NAV  POSN
```

PLOTTING THE POSITION

This position is in the English Channel south of
Portland Bill, and traditional navigators accustomed to
taking data from several sources will put it on the chart
by reference to the latitude in line two and the longitude in line three. Figure 5 shows how it is done with a
parallel ruler. The navigator starts by finding the mark
for fifty degrees and twenty minutes on the left-hand
scale and, after going up two spaces and a third of the
way up the next space after 50° 20'N, dots in a third of a
minute. He then lays the ruler along the marked line of
latitude below it on the chart. He moves the ruler
upwards, taking care to keep it from skewing on the
paper, and when one edge touches the pencil mark
draws in a line of latitude – the dotted line in Figure 5.
Similarly, using the scale on the bottom of Figure 5,
he dots in the place on the scale represented by

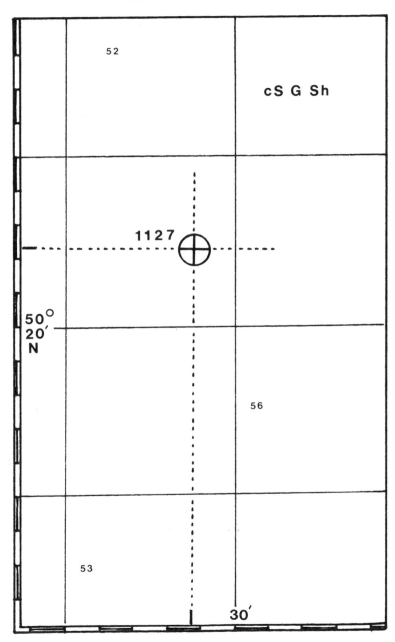

Fig 5. Plotting a fix.

2° 31.245'W and aligns his ruler to the longitude line on the chart. Moving carefully across with the ruler pressed down, he comes to the dot and draws in the line of longitude to cross that of latitude. Where these lines intersect is the fix – the position at the time the Garmin reading was taken – and he now circles the intersection to show that it *is* a fix, and enters the time alongside.

The process is even easier when using a Breton plotter. These useful instruments have a median line at a right angle to the edges, and by sliding the plotter up or along the side or foot of the chart until the median line is on the pencilled dot, you can then put another dot at the other end of the line. Using any straight-edged accessory, a drawn line passing through both dots can be taken to wherever it is needed on the chart and a second line gives the intersection, and hence the fix. This GPS-provided position may be combined with information from other sources to set a course, update a plot, or check on tidal drift or leeway – although experienced and confident GPS users will employ the machine for the purpose to be described in due course.

CURRENT SATELLITE STATUS

Just as most people want to know what the weather is going to be like today or tomorrow, so yachtsmen seek to establish if the GPS set will perform well or not, and the various sets are programmed to provide information on a current or a future basis. The current position is found with the Echostar by touching $\boxed{\text{PWR}}$, then GPS on the softkey, and SATELLITE STATUS on the same softkey. The screen tables the data for five satellites with their azimuths (directions), elevations (heights above the visible horizon) and level (strength of signal in terms of signal-to-noise ratio or SNR). The top half of the page will look like this:

SATELLITE STATUS

SAT NO	12	02	08	14	05
AZM	NW	NE	SW	S	NE
ELEV	21	27	31	26	22
LEVEL	97	58	81	86	61

ELEVATIONS over 15° give the best fixes, and high numbers are desirable on the LEVEL line. The AZIMUTH letters show that the satellites are mostly well spread, and although satellites 02 and 05 are in the same quadrant and not particularly strong, the other three are giving fairly powerful signals likely to lead to a good fix. The bottom part of the same page has the HDOP box, and you will remember from Chapter 1 that a low Horizontal Dilution of Precision number means good geometry, and hence good fixes. The box says:

HDOP	ALL
1.2	16

The low HDOP of 1.2, seen in conjunction with the other data at the top of the screen, indicates that a high-quality signal is available at present.

The Magellan has a simple format showing Geometric Quality (GQ) and Signal Quality (SQ). Touch ON/OFF, wait for READY, and press POS. The first display has latitude and longitude, altitude and mode. A ▽ brings up date and time, while another ▽ discloses status. The page gives the GQ and SQ for each numbered satellite, and looks like this:

```
POS                    GQ  =  7
SAT      03    06            11
SQ        7     4             9
                             ↓
```

The downward arrow at the bottom right-hand corner is an invitation to touch ▽ again to return to the POS display you started with.

The Garmin that gave SQ in bar chart form on the first page of this chapter reveals fuller information with a touch of the STAT softkey at the bottom right on the bar chart display. That brings up:

```
DOP   2.0              EPE         49ft

03  178°  29°  5    23  332°  68°  8

12  127°  10°  1    26  045°  26°  4

17  113°  73°  8    28  300°  27°  4

21  282°  37°  5


         BAR      AUX      SKY    STAT
```

which gives azimuths in the second column and elevations in the third, the DOP figure and the EPE – Estimated Position Error. A touch on the SKY softkey brings a visual display with satellites 23 and 17 high up and central – just as column three indicates in the table – while satellite 12, always a weak satellite as a result of its position on the bar chart and its low figure in the fourth column of the table, is 'black-boxed' as fairly useless in the visual display.

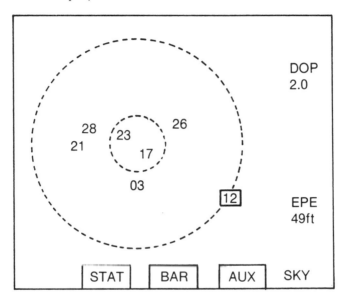

USE OF STATUS DATA

Provided that the set is giving good fixes on demand, most users will not be greatly concerned about status, but there are occasions when knowledge of elevation and azimuth will shape actions. Some sets are programmed not to accept or search for signals from satellites below 10° above the horizon, and this is called the mask angle. High land will create its own mask angle, as Figure 6 shows. The yacht has three satellites potentially of use, but the one on the left is masked by the mountain. An examination of the table would reveal a need to move the

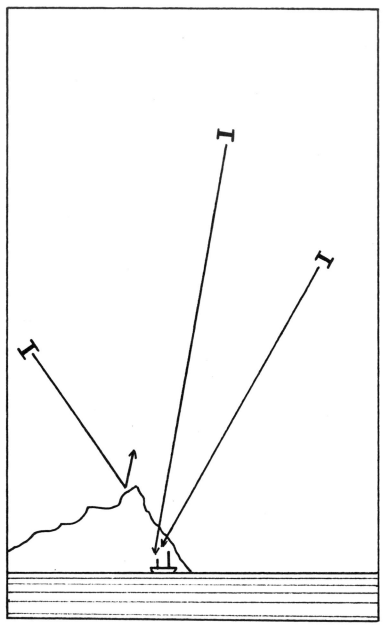

Fig 6. Mask angle from high land.

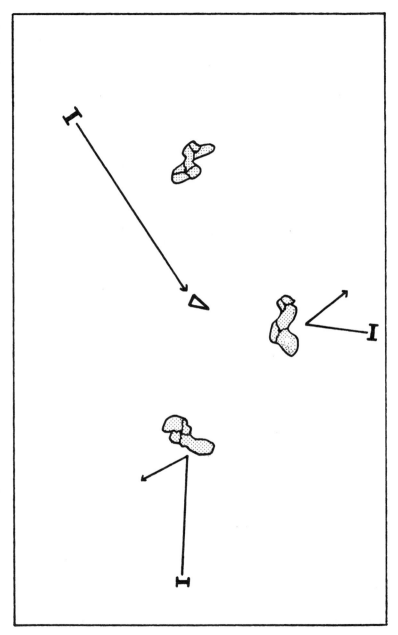

Fig 7. Masking from islands.

yacht further seaward so as to get a decent signal from
that satellite. Similarly, in Figure 7 we can see that
although three satellite signals *should* be available, the
island peaks are blocking two of them and a move of a
mile or two to the south-east or north-east, or a wait of
three minutes, will improve reception on slightly different azimuths. Finally, there is the matter of unhealthy
satellites. Some sets, like the Apelco, will automatically
exclude them, but with others you may have to search
through the status list to see if they are, for example, ON,
TEMP OFF or OFF.

FORECASTS

The Global Positioning System is occasionally fallible, for
it can be switched off, individual satellites may become
unhealthy, and others may be temporarily unreliable. A
bit of homework will pay off on these occasions, and
some sets allow you to check future status. With the
Admiral, you start with POS to get the Sky Plot, and
then by pressing GPS several times a graph of accuracy
predictions appears that holds good for 24 hours. With
this set, you may also enter a date in the future and then
go to POS and several presses of GPS to get a forecast.
The page containing this prediction will have, in its lower
half, a display showing the number of satellites, the mask
angle and the times when they are available for a fix.
When the number of potential satellite signals is reduced
for some reason, you should always make a search before
casting off and leaving harbour.

5 Going places

WAYPOINTS

Waypoints are positions you want to get to, and because repeatable accuracy is the cornerstone of GPS operation it is important that they can be stored in a unit's memory for further use. Waypoints are positions in terms of latitude and longitude and are recorded either by name or number. They can be entered in the memory by the operator who has taken them from a chart, a bearing and distance, a list or an almanac, or they are fixes that have been accepted by the machine as instant waypoints. Often, a fix at a turning point on a voyage is noted as a waypoint for the return journey, while the position from which the voyage starts can be Waypoint One, or HOME or any designation you like. Before we start on a one-leg voyage it is necessary to explain that a GPS set is not at all worried that a prospective trip is between a land position and one at sea; it is programmed to give direction, distance and speed, and doesn't care what lies beneath the paths it charts. For that reason, be wary of letting GPS units linked to automatic pilots start work in rivers or restricted inshore locations, because they look for straight-line solutions to problems and will take no heed of mudbanks, rocks or anchored ships that might be in the way.

THE ONE-LEG VOYAGE

When you are at home, practise by seeking to go from the back garden where the signals are coming in over the hedge to a position off St Catherine's Point on the south-

ern tip of the Isle of Wight. You turn on a hand-held
Magellan and touch $\boxed{\text{POS}}$, and after a short interval the
page looks like this:

```
┌─────────────────────────────────────┐
│                                     │
│     POS            2D               │
│      51°      15.255N               │
│     001°      37.370W               │
│               160f EL               │
│                                     │
└─────────────────────────────────────┘
```

Pause here for a moment. The entry '2D' at top right
means that *three* satellites are giving a fix, and it's reason-
ably reliable. The elevation of 160 feet at bottom right
was put in by you at the initialization stage described in
Chapter 3 and the set hasn't been used anywhere else
since. Touch $\boxed{\text{ENTER}}$ $\boxed{\text{ENTER}}$ and your present position
is fixed as Waypoint One. It appears on the page hereafter
whenever $\boxed{\text{WPT}}$ is pressed and the right-facing arrow
touched to scroll through all those listed in order as:

```
┌─────────────────────────────────────┐
│                                     │
│   WPT 001      51°   15.255N        │
│               001°   37.370W        │
│    2D                160f EL        │
│                          ↓          │
│                                     │
└─────────────────────────────────────┘
```

The destination waypoint can also go in with $\boxed{\text{WPT}}$
$\boxed{\text{ENTER}}$ $\boxed{\text{ENTER}}$, and when keying it will be necessary to
change the elevation as a yacht off the Isle of Wight is *not*
going to have an antenna 160 feet high. Each line of figures for the latitude and longitude will be followed with
an $\boxed{\text{ENTER}}$, and you will $\boxed{\text{CLEAR}}$ the 'old' altitude
before putting in the new. The page should now read:

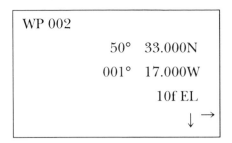

WP 002

50°   33.000N

001°   17.000W

10f EL

↓ →

THE WAYPOINT CHECK

This is going to be one of the shortest sections in the book, but it is here to emphasize that you must *always* check that a waypoint entry into the memory has been successful, because if you don't the whole string of data you may be relying on will have a missing bead. With the Magellan, for example, the waypoint check runs $\boxed{\text{WPT}}$ $\boxed{\triangleright}$ $\boxed{\triangleright}$ with as many right-going arrows as is needed. In this instance the unit will reproduce WP 001, WP 002 and then WP 001 again. The two waypoints *are* entered in the memory and will only be removed when you want to 'dump' them in a manner to be described at the end of the chapter.

MAKING A SHORT ROUTE

To get a course and distance between the two waypoints is to make a short route, and going from WP 001 to WP 002 is by way of $\boxed{\text{ON/OFF}}$ $\boxed{\text{ROUTE}}$ $\boxed{\triangledown}$ to scroll to the next or, in this case, the first route. An $\boxed{\text{ENTER}}$ gives POS and then an $\boxed{\triangleright}$ brings up WP 001. $\boxed{\text{ENTER}}$ produces TO, and an $\boxed{\triangleright}$ again gives another POS and then $\boxed{\triangleright}$ $\boxed{\triangleright}$ once more displays both waypoints. $\boxed{\text{ENTER}}$ $\boxed{\text{ENTER}}$ gives the course in degrees and the distance in nautical miles as:

```
┌─────────────────────────────────────┐
│                                     │
│   WP 001      To      WP 002        │
│                                     │
│   168°M              44.16NM        │
│                                     │
└─────────────────────────────────────┘
```

CHECKING THE RESULT

In the learning stage it is best to check your working, and
with the Magellan this is done by using one of the auxiliary functions. The idea is to feed in the distance and
bearing just obtained to bring up the destination waypoint in terms of latitude and longitude. If the answers
match, you've got it right, and the check starts with:

until WAYPOINT PROJECTION appears. Touch
⎡ENTER⎤⎡▷⎤ so that WP 001 is displayed; this, of course, is
present position. ⎡ENTER⎤ it and key in the distance first,
44.16 nautical miles. ⎡ENTER⎤ these numbers and key in
the bearing figures, 168. A last ⎡ENTER⎤ displays:

   50° 33.047N   001° 17.212W

which is very close to the position selected for WP 002
which was:

   50° 33.000N   001° 17.000W

A ONE-LEG VOYAGE TO A POSITION WHOSE LATITUDE AND LONGITUDE IS UNKNOWN

The WAYPOINT PROJECTION function can be
employed to plot a course to a position without consult-

ing the chart. Let us say that a navigator of a yacht bound for the Canaries wants to turn south at a point 50 miles west of his present position off Ushant. By keying either:

AUX 9 ENTER   or   AUX ▷   × 9

he arrives at a message reading WPT PROJECTION SELECT YOUR POSITION. A POS selects present position and ENTER ENTER a waypoint. The display moves to the distance message; you tap in 5 0 . 0 0 and ENTER it. Key in the bearing, which will be 2 7 0 and ENTER that as well. The unit will now show the destination waypoint plus the bearing and distance entered, and a final ENTER ENTER will confirm and number the waypoint. The route procedure is just the same as when voyaging between WP 001 and WP 002 and described just now, and you have not had to look at the chart at all.

SIMULATION AND THE ONE-LEG VOYAGE

Two of our sets, the Garmin and the Echostar, can operate in simulator mode so that you can practise at home during the long winter evenings. To arrive at this mode with the Garmin, touch the AUX softkey at the foot of the page to get the auxiliary menu and then select Operating Mode and press CLR when at simulator. Thereafter, the page will bear the words 'Simulating Navigation' at the top. The Echostar begins with PWR and MODE , so that three choices present themselves. The softkeys are labelled GPS, FISH FINDER and PLOT, and touching:

FISH FINDER   FISH FINDER   O/SF

reaches the special functions menu. SIMULATOR MODE
ON/OFF is opposite the top softkey, and press this to
change OFF to ON. All subsequent displays will have SIM
on them. Commence practice with the Echostar by
MODE MODE and a softkey selection of GPS and NAV-
IGATE so that the next display has the present latitude
and longitude on it, plus depth, speed and surface water
temperature, although these last items are of little inter-
est at this stage. You decide that to blot out the winter
scene outside you will go from an imaginary position off
the coast of Florida to Gun Cay in the Bahamas, a little
over 50 miles away, and that the waypoint for the destination is at 25° 33.41'N, 79° 18.89W with the code name
BACON.

A touch on MODE and STORE/LIST WAYPOINT
brings up a message – ENTER NEW WAYPOINT?
Another touch reveals STORE WAYPOINT and an invitation to enter the code name of the destination. This is
accomplished by using the right and left arrows to
change lettering, with the keying going something like:

B ADD A ADD C ADD O ADD N ADD ENT

Next comes a display with choices, including the invitation to STORE WAYPOINT BY LAT/LONG. Press the
softkey, and follow the instruction to ENTER YOUR LAT-
ITUDE. The keying is:

2   5   3   3   4   1   ENT

followed by the longitude:

7   9   1   8   8   9   ENT

Touch GO TO WPT LIST and WPT 1 appears as:

> BACON   N   25° 33.41
>   W   79° 18.89

STOR puts it by for future use. With this set, present position is always Waypoint Zero and, as we shall see, the numbers of the instant waypoints from present position start at 80 and run to 99.

GETTING TO BACON

Once the Echostar has the waypoints, the rest is relatively simple. The navigation page is found from:

> MODE   GPS   NAVIGATE

and a press of GOTO 0 1 ENT brings up a second-line message reading:

> 01   BRG   DTG
>   BACON   58°   52.9ML

with the bearing, or course, as 058°M and the Distance To Go just under 53 miles.

RETURNING TO STARTING POINT

To come back from BACON to present position, touch the 1/EVENT key. A message will appear at the bottom right of the page to say EVENT 80 SAVED, and this tells you that the starting point is now Waypoint Eighty. GOTO 8 0 ENT gives bearing and distance. These temporary or instant waypoints are expendable, and we will go back to using the Magellan to show how they are got rid of when surplus to requirements.

DUMPING WAYPOINTS

Having toiled over the keys to acquire waypoints, it is an irony that we soon have to get rid of some of them, or even all of them, to make room for more. The Magellan has a fast track item for the purpose. By keying:

the ALL WPTS ERASED message appears. To drop just one waypoint, you first find it by scrolling through with ROUTE and ▷ to come to the one due for the chop. Let us say we get to:

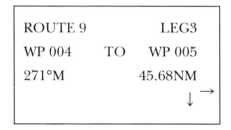

and want to remove Waypoint Five. A press of ENTER takes out the *destination* waypoint. If, on the other hand, you wanted to dump Waypoint Four it would be necessary to scroll on, or back, to the WP 003 to WP 004 page to get rid of the latter with an ENTER

The Apelco works in a different way. Select the mode with a touch of WAYPT and a number display appears. Choose the number due for eradication and press ENTER CLEAR CLEAR so that 'Ent to Erase' comes up on the page. If you now touch ENTER , the set will dump it and return to POS. If, on the other hand, you feel inclined to mercy at this late stage, an EXIT will provide a reprieve.

The Apelco GXL 1100 unit.

6 The waypoint directory and making a route

WAYPOINT DIRECTORY

Some old-timers keep tattered notebooks with lists of waypoints, and this is probably a habit from the days when Loran C and Decca sets were in their infancy and information was stored in this way. Machine storage is more efficient, and with the Echostar the routine is an easy one. First, to deal with finding a waypoint, which starts by entering the directory with:

PWR MODE GPS and touching STORE/LIST
WAYPOINT and GOTO WPT LIST using

the △ and ▽ buttons to scroll through. We are looking for our old friend BACON, and as you go down #3 (blank) #2 (blank) you come to:

#1	BACON	N 25° 33.41
		W 79° 18.89

Now for Waypoint Eighty, and the scrolling goes #77 (blank), #78 (blank), #79 (blank), and then:

#80	N 25° 02.80
	W 79° 57.00

shows up. Having found it, the GPS user decides that it needs to be transferred to the permanent list, and this is done with a press of the SAVE softkey and following the instruction to COPY WAYPOINT by entering 8 0 and touching the COPY softkey. It *should* now be in the permanent directory with a new number, but let's check to be sure. Go back to MODE , STORE/LIST WAYPOINT and GOTO WPT LIST on softkeys and look at the list. It should now read:

1	BACON	N 25° 33.41
		W 79° 18.89
2		N 25° 02.80
		W 79° 57.00

and the new number may be supplemented by a code name – perhaps GUNK for Gun Cay will do – to make it more memorable.

USING THE DIRECTORY FOR NAVIGATION

The waypoint directory will give courses and distances between waypoints very readily without any use of POS, and an example follows of the return trip from the new Waypoint Two to BACON. Go to MODE and GPS, then touch the softkeys for STORE/LIST WAYPOINT and GOTO WPT LIST as before, but this time scroll to a blank place before touching the SAVE softkey. MEASURE WAYPOINTS is the next softkey, and the page will reveal:

MEASURE WAYPOINTS   WPT FROM   WPT TO
                          .

so that entering 0 2 and 0 1 calls up a bearing and distance of 238° and 52.9ML. Note here that 238° is the reciprocal of the 058° course for going the other way outlined in the last chapter, while the DTG is the same – 52.9ML. A CLR will enable further calculations to be made, and an ENT takes you back to the waypoint list for more data.

The Trimble NavTracXL holds 99 routes and 500 waypoints in its memory.

MAKING ROUTE – PRELIMINARIES

A route is a pre-planned sequence of one-leg trips between waypoints sewn together, and is useful to the navigator when the voyage has a number of changes of course. Typically, a route is employed when the yacht is running along a coast from headland to headland or weaving through an archipelago. Most sets can cope with routes containing between ten and twenty courses and distances in their memories. Naturally, you have to have the waypoints first and, although I said earlier that note-books with lists of waypoints are not a good idea, it can be very helpful to have waypoint and route working sheets in a folder so that a rough log may be kept of the voyage and the data is available for next time. In the case

Waypoint and Route Working Sheet

No	Name	Desc	Lat	Long	Log	Time	Brg	Dist
002	CAPO	Off St Catherine's Point	50° 33.000N	001° 17.000W				
003	BILL	Off Portland Bill	50° 25.000N	002° 27.000W				
004	STAR	Off Start Point	50° 10.000N	003° 45.000W				
005	FALMO	Off Falmouth	50° 06.050N	004° 56.000W				
006	LIZ	Off Lizard Point	49° 56.000N	005° 12.000W				
007	WOLF	South of Wolf Rock	49° 55.000N	005° 48.000W				

of a sailor who makes annual trips down-Channel to the
West Country, the waypoint and route working sheet will
look like the grid on page 47.

Note that the actual geographical location is never
given as a waypoint, for in fog and rain it is all too easy to
hit the land if no one is keeping a good lookout. The
four columns on the right are for keeping a navigational
record; if a ringbinder is used, it makes it easy when at
home to prepare and add routes for use at sea from pho-
tocopies kept on the boat. Preparation of the route varies
with each GPS set, so we'll follow two examples.

MAKING A ROUTE WITH A HAND-HELD MAGELLAN

You will remember that WP 002 is already in the memory
because it was where we went from the back garden in
Chapter 5, and putting in WP 003 begins with:

| ON/OFF | | WPT | | ENTER | | ENTER |

so that the letters 'WP 003' appear on the page and a cursor begins to flicker invitingly. Key in:

| 5 | | 0 | | 2 | | 5 | | 0 | | 0 | | 0 | | ENTER |

| 0 | | 0 | | 2 | | 2 | | 7 | | 0 | | 0 | | 0 | | ENTER |

and touch WPT and ▷ to make sure it has gone in cor-
rectly. Go on with another WPT and key in 004 and 005
from the waypoint and route working sheet. Make a final
check with WPT and some ▷ s. The route is entered,
and we will use it to voyage from WP 002 to WP 005 –
that is, from a point south of the Isle of Wight to a point
off Falmouth.

USING THE ROUTE – MAGELLAN

Start with ROUTE . If WP 002 is already in place on the left of the page, touch ENTER ; if not, scroll with ▷ until it is and press ENTER . The words 'WP 002 TO – ' appear. Scroll on with the right-facing arrow until WP 003 appears, and confirm it with an ENTER . The display changes to 'WP 003 TO – ' and you move on to ENTER WP 004. Similarly, when WP 004 occupies the page, you ENTER WP 005. A second ENTER will bring up the magnetic course and distance from waypoint to waypoint, starting with 265° and 45.25 miles from WP 002 to WP 003. Put it on the working sheet and ▷ forward to get the remaining courses and distances. When you have them all, the top half of the working sheet will be like the table on page 51.

At this point you have a choice of using automatic or manual mode, and we'll cover the automatic mode first because it is the norm. (The Magellan unit arrives from the makers equipped with this setting.) Make a check with SETUP ▽ ▽ ▽ to make sure you are on AUTO MAG (M) and that the automatic route mode is in operation. In this automatic mode the message CLOSE is displayed when the yacht comes within 500 feet of the next waypoint, and when it arrives at the centre of that circle the page shifts automatically to the next leg. So, at the end of the leg between WP 002 and WP 003 the 265° courseline changes to a new courseline of 259°. Figure 8 may make this clearer, because it shows a line at right angles to the original courseline where the shift takes place. If the manual mode has been used, the set will show ARRIVED, and you must key in ROUTE and ▷ to move forward to the next leg.

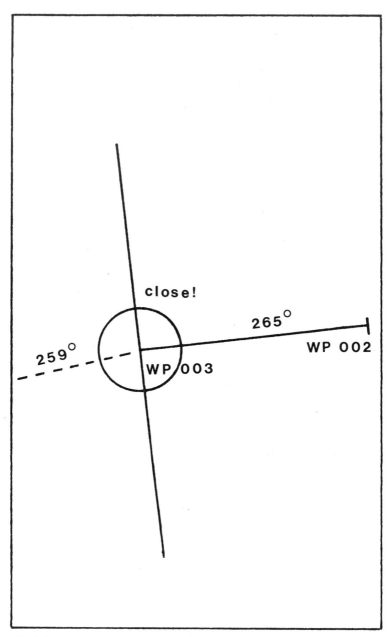

Fig 8. The arrival circle.

Waypoint and Route Working Sheet

No	Name	Desc	Lat	Long	Log	Time	Brg	Dist
002	CAPO	Off St Catherine's Point	50° 33.000N	001° 17.000W			265°	45.25
003	BILL	Off Portland Bill	50° 25.000N	002° 27.000W			259°	52.04
004	STAR	Off Start Point	50° 10.000N	003° 45.000W			271°	45.68
005	FALMO	Off Falmouth	50° 06.050N	004° 56.000W				

MAKING A ROUTE – ECHOSTAR

Start with GPS   ROUTE/SET ALARMS   MAKE ROUTE
on the softkeys and a table appears so that route numbers may be assigned. As this is the first one, the cursor
stays where it is on RTE 01. MAKE brings up the MAKE
ROUTE page with the waypoint list on it. We are doing
the same journey as before and seek a route running
from WPT 2 to WPT 5 and, as it happens, four waypoints
is the maximum the screen will take without scrolling for-
ward or back with $\triangle$ or $\triangledown$. The entries are INC $\boxed{0}$ $\boxed{2}$,
with 02 appearing in the WPT NO square under OR, fol-
lowed by $\boxed{\triangleleft}$ INC $\boxed{0}$ $\boxed{3}$ $\boxed{\triangleleft}$ and $\boxed{\triangleleft}$ INC $\boxed{0}$ $\boxed{4}$ $\boxed{\triangleleft}$ INC
$\boxed{0}$ $\boxed{5}$ $\boxed{\triangleleft}$. Now return to MODE   ROUTE/SET ALARMS
and LIST ROUTE to see that it is all properly recorded.
The top line should show:

	FIRST	LAST
RTE 01	# 02 C	# 05 F

and indicates that the route is in the memory.

USING A ROUTE AND FOUR WAYS OF REVERSING IT

To use this route, start with $\boxed{\text{MODE}}$ and touch
ROUTE/SET ALARMS and SELECT ROUTE. Bring the
cursor on to RTE 01 and press AUTO. This ensures that
the unit will switch automatically to the next leg when
the arrival alarm position is reached. Reversing the route
is easy with the Echostar because this set has a REV softkey that will bring WPT 5 from the memory as first leg
starting point on the way back. The Magellan has more
key-strokes for a reversal of route, and you have to touch
$\boxed{\text{ROUTE}}$ $\boxed{\text{AUX}}$ $\boxed{\triangleright}$ $\boxed{\triangleright}$ $\boxed{\text{ENTER}}$ and then scroll through

with $\boxed{\nabla}$ to get the route number. When it is displayed, an $\boxed{\text{ENTER}}$ will produce the message – ROUTE REVERSED. The Apelco gets you to display the route, and $\boxed{\circlearrowleft}$ $\boxed{\text{ENTER}}$ will reverse it, while the Garmin employs $\boxed{\text{AUX}}$ $\boxed{7}$ $\boxed{\text{ENTER}}$ followed by the scrolling downward arrow to find the words REVERSE ROUTE 1. An $\boxed{\text{ENTER}}$ does the trick, and touching any key *except* ENTER enables you to leave the reverse route function. If, of course, you want to end-for-end more than one route, the down arrow on the Garmin will take you to the next one requiring reversal. We started with a sailor who went up and down Channel each year, and he or she will want to keep this route in the unit from year to year. The lithium battery will preserve the information intact even though the set is unplugged and taken home each winter or, in the case of a hand-held set, the torch or shaver batteries are removed.

7 Cross track error and the course to steer

The waypoints and the routes give us the way we *ought* to go, and if all our voyages took place on a lake on a still day nothing more would be needed. The bearing that the unit has given is just a courseline – a planned direction of travel – but wind, wave and current will be acting together to drive the boat off that courseline; therefore, making corrections is a constant chore. Let us see how the various sets cope with them, and keep an eye on Figure 9 which explains the terms used.

CROSS TRACK ERROR CORRECTIONS WITH THE ADMIRAL

A NAV leads to a display showing range and bearing to the waypoint, plus other items including four softkey options. One of them is STEER, and a touch reveals the page below:

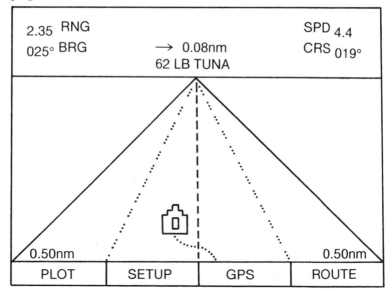

The centre dotted line is the courseline, and the cursor that looks a little like a mini-castle is your craft. It is to port of the courseline, so that a turn to starboard is indicated. Range to the waypoint, its bearing, the speed and present course are given at the top of the page. Top centre is an arrow showing that a turn to starboard is needed; the accompanying figure shows that the craft is just 0.08 of a nautical mile off the courseline, and that is a mere 150 metres or so. The waypoint is about two and a third miles away according to the figure in the top left-hand corner of the page, and the important thing in this case is *not* to overreact. A change of direction of perhaps three degrees to starboard will suffice, and as you go on the cross track error (XTE) reading of 0.08 should decrease. If it doesn't, give it another couple of degrees until there's a fall in the value. The cursor will be of assistance when other matters claim attention and the odd check of XTE is required.

CROSS TRACK ERROR CORRECTIONS WITH THE ECHOSTAR

This set has a Course Deviation Indicator (CDI) of a slightly different type, but the centre line has the same function: it is the courseline or track line. The page is arrived at by:

⬚ PWR ⬚   ⬚ MODE ⬚   GPS   NAVIGATE   CDI

and looks like this:

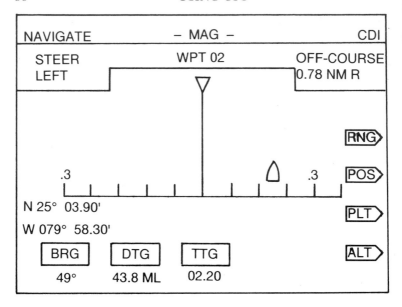

The Echostar display shows that the vessel is off-track to starboard, and the figure is about three-quarters of a mile. Top left is the advice to STEER LEFT, and at the foot of the page is the Distance To Go (DTG) and the Time To Go (TTG). For present course and speed you must touch the ALT softkey, while a second ALT will supply Course Made Good (CMG) – the direction you are actually going, as opposed to that envisaged by the machine. The RNG softkey enables the user to change the scale, which at present gives a third of a mile for each division away from the central courseline. As before, a few degrees to port will bring the ship-shaped cursor back towards the central line and the XTE figure will diminish. What do you do if you are a considerable distance off the courseline? Basically, you start again, using POS as a waypoint and entering the destination waypoint as for a one-leg voyage.

TERMS EXPLAINED

This is a good time to get some of the terms used in the manuals sorted into categories, for manufacturers tend to employ words supplied by the boffins with minimum explanation. Look at Figure 9 and run through it from the bottom. BRG[1] is the magnetic bearing supplied by the unit to get from WP 02 to WP 03. Halfway up is the XTE caused by the wind blowing from the west and pushing the boat off the courseline to the east. At the moment the amount of XTE is established, the Distance Made Good (DMG) is represented by the line joining WP 02 and the ship, while Course Made Good (CMG) is the angle in degrees between the north pointer and the DMG line. Above the XTE line there is a break put in to show that Velocity Made Good (VMG) is the speed as it would be measured along this piece of courseline from the XTE join to the dotted line, while Speed Over the Ground (SOG) is measured from the ship towards WP 03 and is the *actual* ground speed when the dotted line is reached. BRG [2] is the new courseline for WP 03, and the Course Over the Ground (COG) is put in to show what happens if you don't make enough allowance for XTE. The GPS user has changed course to port, but the wind is still pushing the boat sideways so that the 'new' COG is parallel to the old courseline and another alteration will be needed to close WP 03. Many of the terms that have been coined in recent years use speed and velocity as interchangeable, so that Velocity Over the Ground (VOG) is the same as ground speed, while with the Magellan you actually get SOG if you touch $\boxed{\text{VEL}}$. It is always best to assimilate as many of the manufacturer's meanings for functions as you can before getting down to serious work with an actual set.

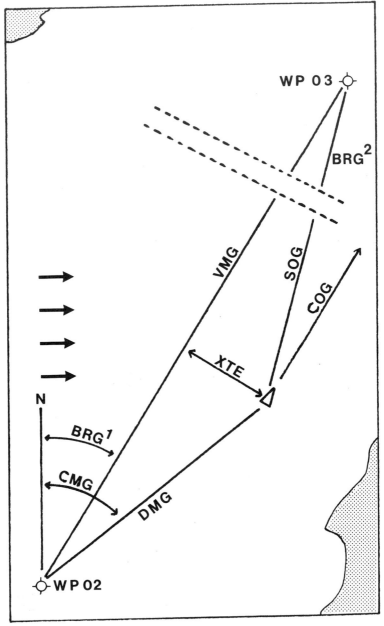

Fig 9. Some terms used in GPS navigation.

OFF-COURSE ALARM – APELCO

On a longish trip, people won't be happy poring over the unit for hours on end to make small course changes, and many sets have off-course alarms to tell you when an alteration must be made. With the Apelco, the technique is to touch:

to select the alarm display and follow up with numbers representing the limit you want to set. Figure 10 has the essentials. The solid line is the track or courseline between two waypoints, and the parallel dotted lines represent alarm or limit boundaries. The navigator wants a half-mile margin and keys:

0		5		0		ENTER

for a half-mile limit, and with the off-course alarm set a beeper will sound if the boat crosses the invisible boundary. To silence the alarm, touch CLEAR, and to cancel the arrangement touch ALARM again and ⟳ ⟳ to get the proper page, and finish with 0 0 0 ENTER so that the cancellation takes effect.

OFF-COURSE ALARM – ECHOSTAR

When on autopilot in the open sea with little shipping about, a more precise limit can be set if, for example, you need to go below for a short time. Go to MODE ROUTE/SET ALARMS   SET ALARMS and select OFF-COURSE. Put in the boundary limits, and in this instance we'll make them 300 yards each side of the track or courseline. Touch:

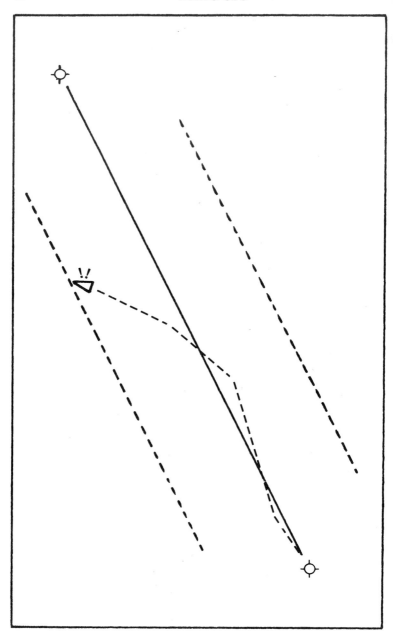

Fig 10. Crossing the XTE alarm line.

OFF-COURSE $\boxed{0}$ $\boxed{1}$ $\boxed{5}$ $\boxed{\text{ENT}}$

and the alarm is set. To silence the bleeper, press $\boxed{\text{CLR}}$, and to cancel the alarm touch OFF-COURSE and key $\boxed{0}$ $\boxed{0}$ $\boxed{0}$ $\boxed{\text{ENT}}$ $\boxed{\text{ENT}}$ so that the display changes to the NAVIGATE page. There is a variant of the off-course alarm called the boundary alarm; we'll deal with this in Chapter 9, when the whole range of alarms and alerts will be examined.

Magellan NAV 5000 D hand-held set.

8 Special items

All GPS sets provide position on demand and a bearing and distance between waypoints, but many also embody a special feature as a selling point – *and* to be one up on the sets of their rivals. We sailors benefit from the competition, and this chapter deals with three areas where manufacturers have provided special items for our use, and the number of waypoints and routes that users are likely to need.

LIGHTS AND BUOYS IN THE MEMORY – ADMIRAL

Micrologic's Admiral set has a built-in database with the name, location and characteristics of lights and buoys in a given area. This is in addition to the waypoints put into the memory by the navigator, and when ordering a unit you can specify which area is going to be the venue for the set. The European version, for example, has over 13 000 lights and buoys in the memory; the Pacific database has about half that number. In effect, you have thousands of extra waypoints on call, and the facility can be of the greatest value on a dark and stormy night at sea when a touch on $\boxed{\text{WPT}}$ repeated several times will bring a display giving the nearest light, as follows.

The navigator can call up to twenty of the nearest lights with the plus key, and each is described by latitude and longitude, bearing and distance. As you may imagine, knowledge of this kind is intensely valuable on a final approach when lights and shapes are distorted by background or shore illumination. Use of the plus or

LIGHT	1st closest
[L]	4320 to PP LITTLE RIVER

N	44° 39.000'
W	067° 11.500'

R 13nm	CHAR FL W 6s

RNG 1.22nm	BRG 352° mag

	DBASE		MOVE

minus keys picks out the most useful marks, and a touch on the GOTO softkey produces a NAV display for the final leg. The buoy display works in the same way with [WPT] [WPT] [WPT], and the operator can *add* up to nine lights and thirty-nine buoys to the memory.

ADDING A LIGHTED BUOY TO THE DATABASE

Let us imagine that an owner seeks to enter into the memory a useful channel buoy that he uses regularly. It is located at latitude N 42° 46.312, longitude W 70° 29.671, has a green light that flashes every two seconds, and can be seen for about a mile. (Note here that the entries that follow are alphanumeric – meaning mixed letters and figures – and the full key description is given. With this set, repeated presses are required to get letters into the memory. To show the database page, touch [WPT] [WPT] [WPT] and DBASE on the softkey followed by [CLR] [1ABC] [ENT] to give a number, and then enter the name:

[CLR] [1ABC] [1ABC] [1ABC] [N△W] [3GHI] [3GHI] [N△W]
     [N△W] [1ABC] [1ABC] [1ABC] [1ABC] [ENT]

followed by the latitude and longitude:

CLR	4JKL	2DEF	4JKL	6PQR	3GHI	1ABC
2DEF	ENT	CLR	0	7STU	0	2DEF
9YZ	6PQR	7STU	1ABC	ENT		

and then add the visible distance:

CLR	1ABC	ENT

followed by the light characteristic:

CLR	2DEF	2DEF	2DEF	N⏶W	4JKL	4JKL
4JKL	N⏶W	N⏶W	3GHI	N⏶W	N⏶W	2DEF
2DEF	2DEF	2DEF	2DEF	N⏶W	7STU	ENT

This lighted buoy is now in the memory, and will be displayed on the page with a B symbol when required.

FISH FINDER – ECHOSTAR

This extra is basically an echosounder that provides a variety of depth contour displays because the GPS set comes complete with a transducer and cable. A touch on:

PWR   MODE   FISH FINDER FISH FINDER

brings up a page with combined depth and position data on it, so that the screen shows the bottom with a scale in feet plus digital readouts of surface water temperature, boat speed, latitude and longitude, and log distance for the day. Echoes above the image of the bottom *may* be fish, but they may also be weed or debris. To take a closer look at these images, go back with $\boxed{\text{MODE}}$ to get A-SCOPE and a split screen that reveals the depth on the right and amplified fish echoes on the left. The split display comes into its own when anchoring in a tight spot where the hook has to go in a particular place, or when looking at fish congregating *under* the hull.

When fishing, or when feeling your way along a sandbank or reef, the sounder part of the Echostar can go on automatic adjustment with $\boxed{\text{2/RANGE}}$ $\boxed{\text{2/RANGE}}$ so that it will change scale as needed. To slow down the images when fishing, touch $\boxed{\text{6/C.SPD}}$ and $\boxed{\triangledown}$, and to speed them up do it the other way with $\boxed{\text{6/C.SPD}}$ $\boxed{\triangle}$. The first close-up comes with:

FISH FINDER FISH FINDER $\boxed{\text{O/SF}}$ FISH LOCATOR $\boxed{\text{O/SF}}$

which produces fish-shaped images that may, and may not, be the real thing, while a follow-up with:

$\boxed{\text{MODE}}$ FISH FINDER $\boxed{\text{O/SF}}$ WHITE LINE $\boxed{\text{O/SF}}$

creates a separation line between the fishy images and the bottom. This line can be very useful when anchoring, because it gives a hint as to the nature of the bottom. A wide line means mud or sea-grass, while a narrow one signifies a hard bottom such as sand or rock. The apparent schools of fish can be looked at again with:

$\boxed{\text{MODE}}$ FISH FINDER   FISH FINDER $\boxed{\text{4/ZOOM}}$

which magnifies the left-hand side by four times. There is a zoom bar that may be moved up and down with the four softkeys to cover each quarter of the page. Thus, to look closely at the bottom echoes, use the lowest softkey;

to see what is happening just under the surface, try the topmost softkey.

THE SHALLOW ALARM

Although alarms in general are covered in Chapter 9, the shallow alarm is a useful tool that can be considered here. It has two main functions: to get into the right spot for fish on the edge of a shoal area, and for use when anchoring. To set it, touch:

$\boxed{\text{MODE}}$ FISH FINDER $\boxed{\text{8/ALARM}}$ $\boxed{\triangledown}$

so that an instruction appears bottom right on the page. It will say something like:

```
USE    ▽  /  △   KEY
ALM.S              0
```

and the idea is that if you want, say, to know when the boat is in 20 feet of water, you press the $\boxed{\triangledown}$ key until '20' shows in the number part of the box. An alarm bar at the right edge of the display will also show 20 feet as the end of a black tube. $\boxed{\text{CLR}}$ will turn the buzzer off when the alarm is no longer needed, and the alarm is cancelled altogether when the up or down key returns to zero.

INTEGRAL PLOTTERS

Plotters fall into two categories: those integral to the set; and those that are separate, but linked to a GPS unit. We'll stay with the Echostar for the time being because it has an integral tracking plotter that helps fishermen find wrecks and holes, while sailors can press it into service if they are off the chart, or have forgotten to bring the right one along. The page is arrived at from the PLOT

softkey when in NAVIGATION mode, and it shows the
boat's position as an '+' on the left side with depth data
on the right. Various scales are available, but the 5-mile
one seems to be most used. The '+' moves down the lines
between waypoints, and when it gets to the edge of the
page there is automatic re-centring to put it back in the
middle. (If you want to get back in the centre before
reaching the edge, an ⎡ENT⎤ will fix it.) The waypoint
numbers come up with ⎡3/GOTO⎤ , and if you were seeking to voyage from present position to, say, WPT 66, it is a
simple matter to touch ⎡6⎤ ⎡6⎤ ⎡ENT⎤ so that a dotted
courseline will appear on the plotter showing the way to
the destination. The ultimate in integral plotters is probably the Humminbird NS10 made in Eufaula, Alabama. It
does not need C-MAP cartridges, as do many other
graphic sets, and is designed so that you can do without
waypoints if you wish. With the set switched on, you put
the cursor on the destination and touch ⎡GOTO⎤. Course,
distance and time of arrival appear on the display, while a
solid 'old course history' line tells you where you've
been. The digitized maps it uses are largely derived from
satellite photographs, and are probably more accurate
than most charts. This type of unit will, I believe, make
maximum impact in the years to come.

LINKED PLOTTERS

Linking a GPS set to a plotter is largely a matter of compatibility, and the first essential is to get matching NMEA
numbers. The Magellan, for example, will only work with
one of the NMEA 0183 series, and the keying for a link-
up goes like this. Touch:

⎡AUX⎤   ⎡6⎤   ⎡ENTER⎤   to show

```
┌─────────────────────────────┐
│  NMEA      SETUP            │
│  PORT                      │
│  OFF              →        │
└─────────────────────────────┘
```

and then scroll through with the right-facing arrow to get
to:

```
┌─────────────────────────────┐
│  NMEA      SETUP            │
│  PORT                      │
│  0183A            →        │
└─────────────────────────────┘
```

which should match the NMEA data for the plotter. Of
course, plotters, fish finders and buoy and light lists in
the memory are essentially additional refinements, with
routes and waypoints coming first in importance. The
number of the latter is infinitely variable, so we'll end
this chapter with a survey of what is currently available.
You can then make a mental note as to what kind of set is
best suited to your particular needs.

HOW MANY ROUTES AND WAYPOINTS DO YOU NEED?

Some boatowners will want as many routes and waypoints
as the set will provide; others will require a mere handful.
The memory capacity of ten sets currently available
appears in the table opposite, and these ten are exclusive
of the five featured in this book. As may be seen, the GPS
user who wants a large number of routes and waypoints
will be looking at a set like Trimble's NavTracXL with its
99 routes and 500 waypoints (see page 46), while the
more modest needs of a coasting sailor could be met by

the Streamline ST 400 with three routes and 99 waypoints (see photograph). The sturdy, simplified ST 400 was, at the time of writing, selling at £629; the NavTracXL was more than double at £1 695.

The Streamline ST 400 holds three routes.

Maker and Set	Routes	Waypoints
Trimble NavTracXL	99	500
Raytheon Raystar 390	10	300
Philips ap navigator	20	200
Navstar XR4	9	199
Streamline ST 400	3	99
Garmin GPS 100 EURO	10	250
Humminbird NS 10	99	249
Panasonic KX-G 5500	9	99
Magellan NAV 5200DX	20	500
Trimble Ensign	9	100

9 Alarms and alerts

In passing, we have touched on the subject of off-course and shallow water alarms, and now is the time to run through some of the other alarms and alerts in the menu.

ANCHOR ALARM

As the name implies, this is a device to warn you of a dragging anchor, and the primary message in Figure 11 is *not* to make the alarm circle so small that you are up on deck tending to the anchor and chain whenever there's a puff of wind. In the examples that follow, the tightest alarm circle has a radius of 0.05 nautical miles, or about 300 feet, while Figure 11 shows an outer circle with a sensible radius of 360 feet, which is about right for a boat riding to 20 metres of chain.

ANCHOR ALARM – APELCO

Start with the EVENT key to save the spot where the boat has settled after anchoring as a waypoint, and put it in the memory with GOTO, a number, and ENTER. Touch ALARM and the ⟳ key, and enter the drift limit. Let it be:

0   0   5   ENTER

for the minimum 300 feet. If you drift with the tide, or are blown by the wind outside the circle, the audio beeper will go off and ANC will blink on the page. To silence it, touch CLEAR; to cancel, touch ALARM and

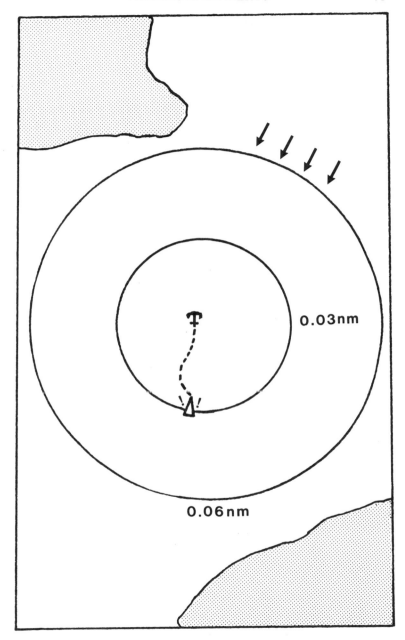

Fig 11. Tight alarm circles make for disturbed nights.

⟳ to get the display, finishing off with ⎡0⎤ ⎡0⎤ ⎡0⎤ ⎡ENTER⎤ so that the unit returns automatically to the NAVIGATE page.

ANCHOR ALARM – GARMIN

The AUX softkey brings up the auxiliary menu, and at ALARMS/CDI the page looks like this:

```
┌─────────────────────────────────────┐
│            ALARMS/CDI                │
│     Anchor:      0.10 n    ▷ on      │
│                       m              │
│                                      │
│     Arrival:     0.05 n    ▷ on      │
│                       m              │
│                                      │
│     Clock:       00.00     ▷ off     │
│                                      │
│     CDI Scale        ▷ +   1.00      │
│                        _             │
│                                      │
│     Steer To         ▷ center        │
│     ┌───────┬─────┬───────┐          │
│     │ PREV  │ AUX │ NEXT  │          │
│     └───────┴─────┴───────┘          │
└─────────────────────────────────────┘
```

with the regular anchor alarm limit of 0.10 of a nautical mile already entered on the top line and the arrival alarm limit (which we'll deal with in the next paragraph) of 0.5 of a nautical mile on the next line. ⎡ENT⎤ will set the alarms, and a ⎡CLR⎤ gives the cancellation.

ARRIVAL ALARMS

The Garmin arrival alarm, set with an ⎡ENT⎤, will sound when the boat is half a mile from a destination waypoint, and the range can be varied by the user. The Admiral has eight alerts that may be established by SETUP ⎡POS⎤ SETUP, and waypoint arrival is top of the list. Turn on with a ⎡CLR⎤ ⎡ENT⎤ and set the range. This can be a fifth (0.20) of a mile and the figure goes in sandwiched between a CLR and an ENT. On arrival, the beeper sounds and the display gives a visual confirmation.

AVOID ALERTS

These are variants of the arrival alarm, and used when sailing among isolated dangers such as coral reefs and pinnacle rocks just beneath the surface. With the Admiral, the setting might go in as NAV SETUP AVOID, followed by a latitude and longitude and a range. This could be:

0   3   0   ENT

to give a third of a mile warning of the danger. The Garmin has a proximity waypoint page that serves the same purpose, and when you enter the alarm circle around a named danger it will beep and put a message on the page reading 'Prox Alarm Wolf' if, for example, the Wolf Rocks are the danger that has been treated as a waypoint.

BOUNDARY ALARM

The boundary alarm combines the best features of the three alarms previously described, and the technique is to enter waypoints either side of a danger, join them with an imaginary courseline, and put alarm boundaries parallel to that courseline. Figure 12 shows the practical application of boundary alarms to the Wolf Rocks, which run from south-west to north-east in the path of shipping. A waypoint to the south-west at N 51° 05.10', W 12° 43.22' and another to the north-east at N 51° 08.95', W 12° 39.01' span the limits of the reef.

The navigator wants his GPS unit to tell him when he's within half a mile of any danger, and the first task is to

enter the two waypoints. Using an Echostar, the prelimi-
naries are:

[PWR] [MODE] STORE/LIST WAYPOINT ENTER
NEW WPT?

The next number is #03, and the name goes in first as:

[E] (ADD) [G] (ADD) [G] (ADD) [S] (ADD) [ENT]

followed by the latitude and longitude:

[5] [1] [0] [5] [1] [0] [ENT]

[0] [1] [2] [4] [3] [2] [2] [ENT]

and a touch on ENTER NEW WPT? to add:

#4   [P] (ADD) [A] (ADD) [N] (ADD) [ENT] and

[5] [1] [0] [8] [9] [5] [ENT]

[0] [1] [2] [3] [9] [0] [1] [ENT]

with a check on GOTO WPT LIST to make sure both
positions are in the memory.

To make a route between the two waypoints EGGS and
PAN, start with:

[MODE] GPS ROUTE/SET ALARMS MAKE ROUTE

to reveal that this is going to be Route 02. If it's not
already there, put the cursor on RTE 02, and touch
MAKE. The route is going to be from WPT 03 EGGS in
Figure 12 to WPT 04 PAN and the keying continues:

INC 03 [◁]   to   INC 04 [◁]

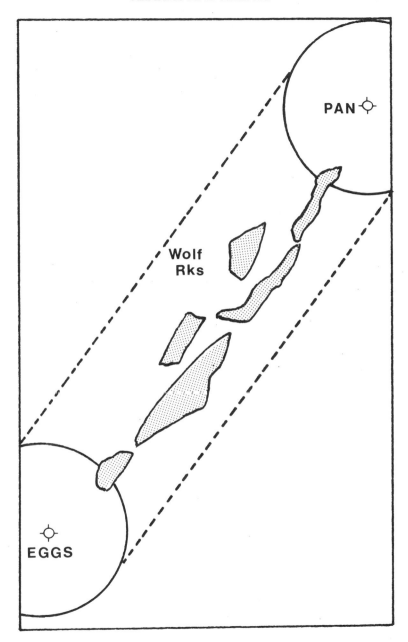

Fig 12. Boundary alarms warning of rocks.

and by checking with MODE ROUTE/SET ALARMS
LIST ROUTE, it can be seen that the route is entered
and ready for use. On touching MODE ROUTE/SET
ALARMS SET ALARMS, the multiple choices include
BOUNDARY, and a touch on the softkey discloses a blank
into which you insert the half-mile limit as 0 5 0 , finishing with an ENT . The dotted boundary lines in
Figure 12 are alarmed, and you complete the protective
shield by adding a proximity or arrival alarm limit of half
a mile for the two waypoints. The sausage-shaped alarm
envelope around the Wolf Rocks is now in place.

MAN OVERBOARD

This alarm feature is often given a great deal of emphasis
in the sales literature, and in some sets a MOB key has
this sole function (although it is more commonly a
secondary task). The Garmin, for example, requires a
double touch on GOTO MOB to record the position
where the crew member went overboard, while the
Admiral records this position with SAVE SAVE . The
Apelco does the same thing with EVENT and GOTO
pressed simultaneously, and most sets will either automatically show bearing and range back to the man overboard
position, or do so at the touch of an ENT . The chief
value of the man overboard feature in GPS sets is that the
position is treated and stored as a waypoint, so that if rescue craft have to be called in to assist with a search following a MAYDAY, they have an accurate position fix to
serve as the centre of a rescue pattern. VHF manufacturers are currently taking the procedure one stage further.
A device called the Emergency Vessel Location System
(EVLS) Mayday Module and an adapted microphone is
fitted to a VHF set connected through a standard NMEA
0183 interface to a GPS set. When a button is pressed on

the microphone the set comes alive, moves to Channel 16, takes the vessel's position from the GPS, and converts the data to a voice pattern via a speech synthesis chip. The distress message is sent, and the GPS set updates the vessel's position continuously so that rescuers know where man overboard took place and where the parent vessel is thereafter. The VHF/GPS combination has been termed Mayday Mike, and we are likely to hear more about it in the future.

10 Accuracy, faults and other uses of GPS

CHARTS AND GPS FIXES

In Chapter 1 there was a preliminary examination of sources of error and standards of accuracy, and in resuming the theme we must start with a recognition that charts printed before GPS existed were based on many different datum positions. It follows that GPS-obtained positions are most accurate with modern charts based on modern surveys, and the top-rank standard is called World Geodetic System 1984, or WGS 84 for short. Your charts may have been purchased fairly recently, but the datum on which they are based could be older. For example, a British chart may bear the legend: 'Positions obtained from satellite navigation systems are normally referred to WGS 72 datum; such positions should be moved 0.05 minutes NORTHWARD and 0.09 minutes EASTWARD to agree with this chart.' However, it would be tedious to change each fix at the plotting stage to correspond with a map datum correction for an earlier method of electronic navigation. Similarly, an American chart purchased in 1992 had a notice reading:

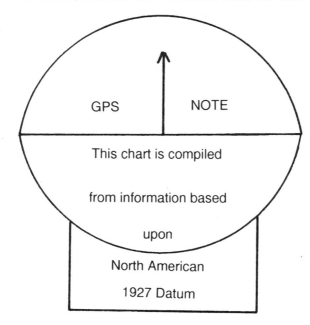

GPS   NOTE

This chart is compiled

from information based

upon

North American

1927 Datum

which is well before electronic position-fixing was a reality. The answer to both these problems is to adjust the readings *from* the set, so that what comes out can go straight on the chart. What happens, though, if you don't make the adjustment? The worst-case scenario is that fixes could be up to 600 metres in error.

SELECTING THE RIGHT MAP DATUM

Most sets have a menu of twelve map datums to match those on charts, and the common ones are:

WGS 84	(often on the set when purchased)
WGS 72	(applicable with earlier electronic systems)
AUSTRAL 66	(Australian waters)
NAD 27	(older American charts)
NAD 83	(American, and the same as WGS 84)

Let us imagine that the set is to be used in Australian waters and the charts give datum as 'Australian Geod 66'. Using a Magellan, a start is made with a down arrow press from the latitude and longitude display to give:

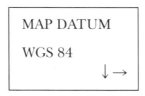

Using repeated presses of the right-facing arrow to scroll through the menu, you come in time to:

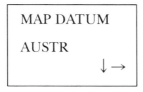

and an· ENTER makes the change.

DIFFERENTIAL GPS (DGPS)

At the end of Chapter 1 there was a mention of Differential GPS as a modification that gave present position with an error of less than 10 metres. It has three elements: a receiver in the yacht capable of processing the data; a beacon to receive it; and a land-based reference station. This station is precisely located, and its equipment can largely negative the effects of Selective Availability by comparing signals received with what it *knows* is right: its present position. The amount of error is transmitted to the differential beacon, and thence to the DGPS set. DGPS has a second function, which is to monitor the health of satellites, and at the time of writing the American GPS Joint Program Office planned to have reference and monitor stations in place by the end of 1995, and the system fully operational a year later.

PRACTICAL APPLICATION OF DGPS

Monitoring stations in the United Kingdom will be funded by private enterprise, so that sailors must pay a subscription for DGPS. Early users are likely to be pilot boats, dredgers, port control units and buoy-positioning authorities, but the private sailor will be able to calibrate a log because the velocity accuracy will be 0.1 of a knot, check compass deviation, obtain accurate time in UTC/GMT for sextant work, or find his or her way to the harbour entrance in the thickest fog. Sets sold as 'DGPS-ready' have a 'D' on the page to show that the signal is a purer one than that obtained under Selective Availability, and the only downside is the extra unit and the royalty fee. In the US, however, it looks as though the Coast Guard will be providing the service at no extra cost.

LATEST DEVELOPMENTS

However, the electronics industry is not putting all its eggs into the DGPS basket, for there are four other trend lines as from 1993. One is to improve signal reception despite Selective Availability, and in Britain the Surbiton-based firm Streamline is working on an eight-channel receiver that will enhance weaker signals and track satellites at low angles below the accepted mask angle limits. On both sides of the Atlantic there are endeavours to add a GPS data input to existing instrumentation, with obvious benefits in space and cost-saving. In the United States, Si-Tex is interfacing a GPS unit with a radar set, so that at the flick of a switch the screen becomes a chart plotter. Networked instruments are the fashion, with a boxed unit uniting several devices, and position, course

Sensor unit for use with the Apelco and Echostar sets.

and distance pass to autopilots and plotters via an NMEA
interface. In Britain, the products of 21st Century in
Whiteparish, Wiltshire, and Marine Electronic Services of
Bristol, are deservedly popular. Chart drums interface
with quite small hand-held GPS units and make use of
paper charts for plotting purposes. Finally, there is more
emphasis on putting working parts into an antenna unit,
as the accompanying photographs will show. The
Echostar and Apelco described in this book get their data
from a sensor and pass it to a display unit. However,
Trimble's Acutis 6 goes a step further. The six-channel
sensor collects and processes the data and then passes it
direct to an existing suite of electronic navigation
devices. The user can upgrade to GPS without replacing
a single item on his or her console, so that this is instant

Acutis six-channel GPS receiver that supplies data to existing instrumentation.

GPS – in every sense of the phrase.

OTHER USES OF GPS

We have looked at GPS solely in a sea navigation context in this book, but it will be helpful to outline other uses. Hikers on a circular ramble over the moor can register the starting position as a waypoint and, when fog shrouds out the landscape, get a bearing and distance back to that starting point at the touch of a button; lake fishermen may return again and again to the spot in the reeds where the 'big 'uns' are lurking; map and chart makers are now revising products based on badly plotted triangulation points or wrongly positioned landmarks; GPS sets are being used to site restaurants and oil wells, locate buried pipelines, and to tell the bulldozer driver where to start his trenching; the thickest jungle and most

FAULT-FINDING	
Problem	*Possible solution*
No power	Check switches and fuses. Are the wires leading to the battery loose? Some sets, like the Echostar, have a 2-amp fuse in the battery lead: check that it hasn't blown.
Dim display	Are the batteries failing? Check the contrast and dim key in case it's *your* fault.
Not receiving	Check satellite status; is the geometry right? Is antenna connected, and does it need repositioning?
Latitude and longitude do not change	Ensure that initialization process has taken. If you are more than two degrees of latitude or longitude from where you switched off, do the start-up routine again.
Constant error in latitude and longitude	Is the HDOP figure wrong at this time of day?
Waypoints, bearings and distances are wrong	Are you on Auto MAG instead of TRUE? Has your boat crossed a meridian so that east/west error may be responsible?
Flashing display	Unreliable for navigation. Switch off and try again later. Check initialization if flashing continues.
Interference	Move antenna; change power source if you can. Switch off other power-users – eg fridges and strip lighting. Check that ground wire is connected. Move set temporarily away from compass.

remote desert regions will cease to be blanks on the map as a result of GPS; and rare animals with collar sets will be tracked in national parks.

One day, a combined GPS set and cellular telephone will enable head office to know that a salesman is on the road and not in the pub, and vehicle-fitted sets and transmitters will enable a transport manager to know where every unit in the fleet is currently located. GPS may be used to control trains, buses and even motorway traffic, so that collision will become virtually impossible. A digitized road map interfaced with a GPS set will guide drivers through busy streets, and the post or zip code will be obsolete and replaced with seventeen numbers that give the location of every building on earth. Crime-fighting could be greatly simplified, with stolen cars broadcasting their whereabouts and a miniature GPS set and transmitter telling the authorities where a prisoner on parole is, and, by inference, what he's up to. So far, the civil liberties lobby has paid little attention to GPS and other satellite location systems, but that may soon change. Right behind the GPS development comes the French system called Spot 3 and its American equivalent named Landsat 6. These satellites photograph as well as locate, and the first use is likely to be finding illegal drug crops and checking that farmers claiming subsidies have in reality planted something. I suspect that just as opposition grew to the tachometer – which was christened the 'spy in the cab' – so will there be murmurings about GPS – the 'eye in the sky'. However, sailors are able to divorce themselves from these considerations, for to them GPS represents the first all-weather, 24-hour positioning prototype, and what follows, be it the Russian Glonass or developments of Inmarsat or Starfix, is certain to be more accurate, less expensive and less dominated by out-of-date military considerations.

Glossary

Acquisition The process whereby the receiving set locates the source of the signal and begins to collect data from the satellites.

Almanac Information as to the location and health of satellites.

Alphanumeric keys Keys that allow the user to enter information in two modes, either as letters or numbers.

Altitude Height of antenna above sea level. Also, see *Elevation*.

Anywhere fix The ability of a receiver to start making position calculations without being given the approximate latitude and longitude, and usually qualified in terms of time.

Auto Mag An automatic adjustment for variation made by a GPS set, so that it delivers magnetic courses and bearings unless told to do otherwise.

Azimuth Bearing of an object in 360° notation.

Bandwidth The range of frequencies in a signal. The bandwidth down which the coded messages pass from satellite to GPS set is a very narrow one.

Black-boxed A frame around a satellite information number indicating that the signal is, or will be, poor.

Clock bias The difference between indicated clock time and Universal Time Coordinated (UTC) or Greenwich Mean Time (GMT).

Coarse (or Course) Acquisition (C/A) C/A is the standard civilian GPS code. The signals received from the satellite are coded and translate into a position fix with a small amount of error.

Control segment Consists of the master control station at Colorado Springs and the other monitor and ground statios throughout the world.

Course Deviation Indicator (CDI) A CDI presents information about cross track error in graphic form.

Courseline The planned line of travel from departure point to destination. A track in orthodox navigation.

Course Made Good (CMG) CMG is the course actually achieved by a craft.

Course Over Ground (COG) COG is the direction of travel achieved, which may not be the courseline.

Course to steer The recommended course to rejoin a courseline.

Cross track error Often printed as XTE or XTK, and representing the perpendicular distance between present position and the courseline.

Cursor Flashing symbol showing where data is to be entered, options changed, or giving the graphic location of the craft.

Department of Defense The American controllers of GPS; often shortened to DoD.

Differential beacon receiver A unit that receives differential signals from coast stations. They are compared to those received from a satellite and the consequent corrections largely reverse the effects of Selective Availability.

Differential Global Positioning System (DGPS) Based on receivers at coast stations supplying signal corrections, it overcomes most of the errors induced by the ionosphere, atmosphere and Selective Availability.

Dilution of Precision (DOP) The measure of quality of satellite geometry, and hence the accuracy of a fix. Also known as Geometric Dilution of Precision and measured on a scale of one to ten. Ten is a poor score; one or two is the best.

Distance Made Good (DMG) Distance from the last position or waypoint to present position.

Elevation Height of antenna above sea level. See *Altitude*.

Emergency Vessel Location System (EVLS) Mayday Module Often abbreviated to EVLS. See *Mayday Mike*.

Ephemeris Data relating to the orbital parameters of satellites.

Estimated Position Error (EPE) EPE is the unit's assessment of the error of a fix in feet.

Estimated Time En Route (ETE) ETE is the time it will take to reach a selected waypoint and is based on Velocity Made Good.

Fix A single position defined by latitude, longitude and altitude.

Geoidal Height The earth is not a perfect sphere, so that a GPS receiver makes an allowance for 'bumps' above the theoretical surface of the earth due to Geoidal Height.

Geometric Dilution of Precision (GDOP) See *Dilution of Precision*.

Geometric Quality (GQ) GQ is another term for Dilution of Precision.

Ground speed Speed Over the Ground as opposed to Speed Through the Water. Velocity Over the Ground is another version.

Horizontal Dilution of Precision (HDOP) HDOP is another term to describe Dilution of Precision.

Initialization Telling the set roughly where it is in terms of latitude and longitude in order to reduce cold-start time.

Ionosphere A band of charged particles encircling the earth about a hundred miles up, which imparts error to satellite signals.

Klutz resistance The built-in ability of the machine to perform properly – despite the clumsiness of the operator.

Leading zeroes Noughts put, for example, in front of a low longitude figure to avoid confusing a machine that is not programmed to accept blank spaces.

Lock When a receiver maintains contact with a number of satellites and can update its position continuously, it has 'lock' on them.

Lock-on time The span of time between switch-on and the reception of a good signal.

Mask angle A satellite is in the mask angle when it is so close to the horizon that a GPS unit gives up the search for it. It also describes the blotting out of a signal by high land.

Mayday Mike A combined VHF/GPS unit that will give a MAYDAY message and the yacht's position at a press of a button.

Nanosecond A millionth of a second.

National Maritime Electronics Association (NMEA) The American organization that sets world standards for compatibility of electronic instruments. For example, a unit bearing an NMEA 0183 label will be compatible with another bearing the same number.

Page The screen on a GPS set.

Protected (or Precision) Code (P-Code) The P-Code is the military version that gives very accurate fixes from transmissions.

Proximity alarm Fitted to sets to tell you that the craft has penetrated the alarm circle put round a proximity waypoint.

Proximity waypoint A waypoint entered to indicate a place to avoid; a danger spot.

Pseudo-random code A succession of noughts and ones transmitted by a satellite and compared to a code at the receiver to give a time difference.

Pseudo-range A distance found from time signals.

Route A sequence of waypoints in order of use.

Satellite Information Number (SIN) The SIN identifies each satellite when status is being determined.

Satellite speed For all practical purposes, satellites move at 1.8 kilometres a second.

Satellite Vehicles (SVs) Satellites are sometimes described as SVs.

Scrolling Repeated pressing of a key to bring up fresh data.

Selective Availability A signal mode that deliberately degrades accuracy by inducing an apparent clock error.

Signal Quality (SQ) SQ describes the strength of signals from a satellite.

Signal-To-Noise Ratio (SNR) See *Signal Quality*.

Softkeys They are often shaped differently, or made of a different material, and frequently placed close to the page with the principal function of making major menu changes. For example, softkeys might be used to change from NAV (for navigate) to SAVE when storing a waypoint.

Space segment The satellite part of GPS.

Speed Of Advance (SOA) SOA is the vector component of ground speed in the direction of the destination waypoint.

Speed Over the Ground (SOG) Often appears as SOG and has the same meaning as ground speed or Velocity Over the Ground.

Standard Positioning Service The level of accuracy achieved with the civil code at Coarse Acquisition standards.

Status A combined assessment made by some GPS sets of the effects of Dilution of Precision and Signal Quality.

Time To First Fix(TTFF) TTFF is the delay in minutes and seconds between switching on and getting a good fix.

Time To Go (TTG) TTG is the estimated time from present position to next waypoint.

Unhealthy A satellite that has developed a fault is declared unhealthy and its transmissions will be ignored by a GPS set.

Universal Time Coordinated (UTC or UT) UTC or UT is an ultra-accurate version of Greenwich Mean Time.

User segment The receivers, processors and antennae that allow an operator to receive GPS signals.

Velocity Made Good (VMG) Speed of closing a selected waypoint.

Velocity Over the Ground (VOG) See *Ground speed* and *Speed Over the Ground*.

Waypoint A position on the surface of the earth that you want to get to, or return to, expressed in terms of latitude and longitude.

Index